MR MEGAMOUTH'S
SHARK
LESSONS

Pickle Hill Primary

Miss Galaxy's Space Lessons
Phil Roxbee Cox

Miss Scorcher's Desert Lessons
Valerie Wilding

Mr Day's Knight Lessons
Phil Roxbee Cox

MR MEGAMOUTH'S
SHARK
LESSONS

Michael Cox

illustrated by
Kelly Waldek

SCHOLASTIC

To Ted and Joyce

Scholastic Children's Books,
Commonwealth House, 1-19 New Oxford Street,
London WC1A 1NU, UK

A division of Scholastic Ltd
London ~ New York ~ Toronto ~ Sydney ~ Auckland
Mexico City ~ New Delhi ~ Hong Kong

Published in the UK by Scholastic Ltd, 2002

ISBN 0 439 99433 0

Typeset by M Rules
Printed by Cox & Wyman Ltd, Reading, Berks

2 4 6 8 10 9 7 5 3 1

Contents

✳ Welcome to Pickle Hill Primary! ✳

Hi, I'm Charlotte Edwards, and before you turn the page, I really need to warn you about a few things. Just in case! I don't want you going in to shock or anything! The thing is, Pickle Hill Primary isn't your ordinary everyday sort of school. It's different. Very different!

For a start, we've got really ace teachers, but the thing is they're all a bit... er... weird! And so are their lessons. Anything can happen in them. You know... like one minute we might be sitting at our desks listening to Mr Megamouth telling us about sharks and the next find ourselves at the bottom of the Pacific Ocean!

Anyway, why not join me and my class, 5M, to hear Mr Megamouth talk about Sharks and then you'll see just what I mean.

by

Charlotte

that's me

Teacher's name: **Mr Megamouth**

Age: Thirty nothing

Appearance: Tall, black hair, with a ginormous pointy quiff. Large white teeth. Grins a lot.

Star sign: Pisces (the fish)

Favourite topic: Anything to do with sharks

Quirks, ticks or odd behaviour:
Dances from one foot to the other when he's excited. Likes to spin around a couple of times when he's pleased with himself.

Information supplied by:
Charlotte Edwards, class 5M

9

The megalodon

Mr Megamouth came into the classroom looking really excited.

"OK!" he said, diving for his pen. "Register time! Let's make it snappy! Today we're going to have an 'in-depth' sharks lesson. It's going to be *fin*tastic!"

He quickly did one of his famous twirls then said, "Did you know that altogether there are about 400 different sorts of shark in the world? Some as small as a cigar and some as big as a bus! They live in all of the world's oceans all the way from the freezing cold poles to the red hot tropics. And they eat everything from plankton to porpoises to lost ship's pussy cats!"

"Ahh!" groaned Kelly Niblett. "Poor pussy cats!"

"Ahh!" said Daniel Mapson. "Poor *poises*!"

And we all burst out laughing!

"Enough!" said Mr Megamouth, suddenly hurling his pen in the air and catching it between his teeth. "Where shall we start?"

"At the beginning?" said Brian Butler. "You know . . . with the very first sharks?"

"Shark thinking, Brian!" said Mr Megamouth. (You get used to the puns after a while.)

"So, how long have sharks been around?" he continued.

"Er, about 10,000 years?" said Kelly Niblett.

"Oh, no, no, *no* . . . Kelly!" cried Mr Megamouth, dancing from one foot to the other. "It's much, much, much *much* longer than that!" Then, seeing she looked a bit disappointed, he said, "Sorry, Kelly. I didn't mean to bite your head off!"

"Er . . . ten *million* years?" said Laxmi Sharma.

"Oh, no, no, *no!*" said Mr Megamouth.

11

Then he paused, smoothed his enormous quiff into an even higher point and said, "But multiply that by 40 and you might be there."

"*Exactly!*" said Mr Megamouth, doing another of his twizzles. "There were sharky type fish swimming the earth's oceans 400 million years ago . . . which is about 200 million years before the first dinosaurs arrived. And 395 million years before the first humans! But sharks like the ones that are around today only began to take shape a mere 64 million years ago, just around the time when the dinosaurs were beginning to die out. Then . . . hey! There's an easier way to do this!"

Mr Megamouth rushed over to his special stock cupboard (the one that *none* of us is allowed into), fished around for a moment, then staggered out with a really ancient-looking film projector. Five minutes later the big classroom blind was down and the funny-looking machine was whirring and clicking into life. As it did, the room emptied of all the everyday stuff like desks and chairs, leaving just us, the contraption and Mr Megamouth huddled in a sort of dark hole! And instead of the moving picture appearing in front of us, it appeared *all the way around* us! Top, bottom and sides! No wonder Mr Megamouth hadn't bothered with a screen. Enormous seaweed waved above our heads, horrible sea creatures swam in front of us, and weird shell things scuttled past our feet. And all the time we could hear that booming, swishing sound you hear when you put your head under the water at the swimming baths. It was brilliant!

"Well, all that sand and rock that you can see beneath our feet will *eventually* be known as California, USA!" said Mr Megamouth. "But not for about another 14 million years. We're on the bed of a gigantic prehistoric ocean. And *it* should be arriving any minute.

"What's *it*?" said Zoe.

"You'll see!" said Mr Megamouth. "Just be patient."

And then we saw *it*! We could just make out a huge, dark shape moving slowly through the murky waters. It had a tail and fins and was absolutely MASSIVE . . . longer than the

Er, where are we, Mr Megamouth?

big bus that brings us to school, *and* wider!

"W . . . w . . . what is it!?" whispered Laxmi.

"It's a megalodon," Mr Megamouth whispered back. "It's a distant relative of the great white shark. But at least a hundred times more dangerous! It's the underwater version of Tyranosaurus rex. Listen! Even though we're in this 'virtuality pod', I'd appreciate it if you'd all keep the noise down. Sometimes the real and the virtual can overlap a little, er, *inconveniently* . . . if you know what I mean!"

We all nodded, then watched the megalodon as it swam towards us.

"Oh dear! I hope things don't start getting too *interactive*!" muttered Mr Megamouth. "Maybe it's time I put the retrojector into reverse!"

But, just as Mr Megamouth reached for the control switch, another huge shape loomed out of the murk.

"Look at *that*!" said Zoe. "Is it *another* megalodon?"

"No," said Mr Megamouth. "It's a prehistoric whale. A young one, though. I think it may have just saved our bacon! Watch."

The megalodon suddenly noticed the young whale and, with a flick of its tail, it turned and dashed at it. The poor thing didn't stand a chance! I won't go into *too* much detail because it was pretty horrible. But the megalodon sort of head-butted the whale and then grabbed hold of it with its massive jaws. The water turned bloody and all sorts of nasty-looking fish swam towards it.

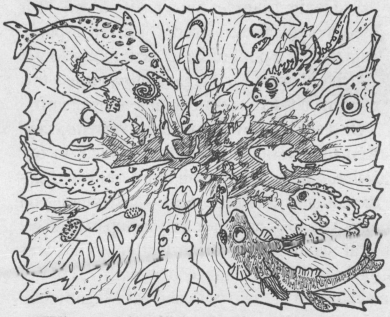

"What are they?" I gasped.

"Prehistoric sharks," said Mr Megamouth.

"They've been attracted by the struggle and the smell of blood. Amazing aren't they!?"

There were sharks with huge spikes along their backs, sharks with horns on their heads, sharks with enormous fins, and sharks that were covered with nose-to-tail "armour-plating"!

These horrible creatures were there for the kill. The whale didn't stand a chance, poor thing. I crossed my fingers and hoped that things just didn't get any more "real".

Suddenly, Liam let out a terrified yell. "Mr Megamouth!" he screamed. "I just felt a splash. And there's a pool of water next to my foot!"

"Uh oh!" said Mr Megamouth. "I knew this machine needed a service! Time we were off!"

He quickly threw the switch on the retrojector. And that was that, we were all back in our classroom, complete with furniture! But that's the thing with Pickle Hill – just when you think you're in one place you end up in another!

"Phwoar!" said Brian Butler. "That was totally brilliant! Can we go again?"

"Hmmm . . . maybe!" said Mr Megamouth, who was busy opening the big blind.

"I definitely did feel a splash!" said Liam.

"And this landed next to my foot."

Now that it was properly light again we could see that Liam was holding a large white object, roughly the size and shape of a giant ice-cream cone. As soon as he saw it Mr Megamouth's eyes almost popped out of his head.

"*That*," he said, "is a megalodon tooth! It must have broken off in the struggle and somehow slipped through the walls of the virtuality pod's time-space interface."

"Yes! Along with all that water!" said Liam, as he put down the tooth and began unlacing his wet trainer!

Mr Megamouth picked up the tooth and held it up for us all to see.

Mr Megamouth laughed, then said, "Do you remember I told you we were in a bit of the Pacific Ocean that would eventually become California? Well, the spot where we were is now known as Shark Tooth Hill. That's because it's now one of the best spots to find megalodon teeth. It's an excavation site where scientists dig up fossils of ancient whales, porpoises, sea lions, turtles and dolphins . . . as well as the teeth of the ancient sharks that terrorized and ate them."

"Do they dig up shark fossils too?" said Daniel.

"Hardly ever," said Mr Megamouth. "The rubbery cartilage skeletons of sharks don't survive like the hard skeletons of bony fish do. So shark fossils are quite rare. But their teeth do last because they're made of hard bony stuff."

"Is it difficult to find the teeth?" said Simon.

"It probably is now," said Mr Megamouth. "But in the old days people used to find them when they were digging . . . or just when they were walking around. They actually believed they were dragons' teeth. Some people even thought they were *thunderbolts* which had been hurled by the thunder gods during storms. By the way, does anyone want to hold the tooth?"

Almost everyone's hand shot up in the air and we all started yelling, "Me! Me! Me!" I got a hold of it in the end.

It's quite heavy, isn't it?

"It came from a very heavy animal," said Mr Megamouth.

"So what would the megalodon have actually weighed then?" I asked.

"No one knows for sure," said Mr Megamouth. "But from the size of the tooth the scientists have worked out that it was probably about 20 tonnes. Which is about the weight of ten cars!"

"That's right!" I said. "It was a *car*nivore, wasn't it!?" And everyone laughed!

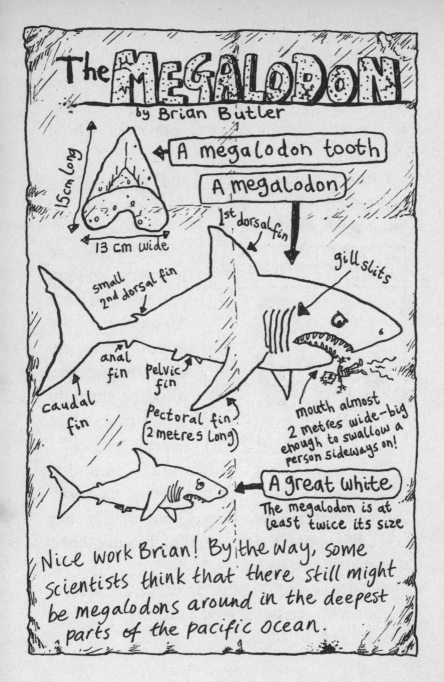

Seymour Oceans

After break, Mr Megamouth reached inside the giant briefcase which he likes to call his "bag of tricks" and took out what looked like a very big bin liner.

"I'd like to introduce you to Seymour Oceans!" he said, holding the bin liner up in front of us. "Seymour is a shark!"

"Looks like a plaggy bag to me," said Daniel.

"That's what *you* think," said Mr Megamouth as he attached the bin liner to a small gas cylinder and flicked a switch. Suddenly the bag began to expand.

"Count to 30!" said Mr Megamouth.

We all began to count, "One, two, three. . ."
When we got to 30, a huge inflatable shark was floating above us!

As we stared up at "Seymour", Mr Megamouth picked up a stick and began pointing out interesting bits about him. "Seymour is a Caribbean reef shark. He's the typical 'rugby ball' or 'torpedo' shape that most people imagine when they think of a shark. But remember, just like children, sharks come in all shapes and sizes. There are flat sharks, long narrow sharks and really weird-shaped sharks."

Daniel looked at Liam and said, "Yes, just like there are really weird-shaped children!"

"Watch it!" said Liam.

Mr Megamouth ran his stick along Seymour's side and said, "Seymour's body is very streamlined. That means it's rounded in front and sort of pointed at the back so that he can whoosh through the water really *smoooothly*! Have you got that?"

"Smoooooooooooooooooooothly!" we all said.

"Hmmm . . . nice!" said Mr Megamouth. Then he twizzled around a couple of times. A moment later he pointed to Seymour's head and said, "Seymour's eyes have a special reflective layer that lets him see in near darkness. But, like most sharks, his eyesight is somewhere between poor and atrocious. He makes up for this with his brilliant hearing though. He can hear low-pitched sounds up to 300 metres away."

But how? He hasn't got any ears!

"Oh yes he has!" said Mr Megamouth. "They're tucked away inside his head. If he *had* got huge great earlobes they'd cause him a problem, wouldn't they?"

"Yes!" said Simon Sidworth. "They'd reduce his aquadynamic efficiency!"

"Slow him down 'an all!" said Kelly Niblett.

"Exactly!" said Mr Megamouth. "And hearing with his ears isn't the only way Seymour detects his prey! Running down each side of him is a row of pressure sensitive points which are known as his lateral lines. They are a bit like a couple of very long thin ears and can detect vibrations coming from tasty creatures that are attempting to sneak past him in murky water. So he *feels* sound as well as hearing it. He can sense vibrations from an injured or struggling fish that's over a *mile* away!"

Ah! I sense dinner!

1 Mile

Victim

Seymour

Seymour's jaws seemed to open, then snap shut again, which was quite clever for an inflatable fish, giving us a very good idea of how deadly his bite was.

"And just to be *entirely* sure that no tasty treats slip by," Mr Megamouth continued, "there are these electro-sensitive jelly-filled holes on Seymour's head. They can pick up the really faint electrical signals that are given off by all living things."

"Poor fish!" said Liam O'Brady. "There's no hiding place for them, is there?"

"Not really," said Mr Megamouth. "And once the chase is on, Seymour's got his powerful tail to push him through the water and give him the speed he needs. Along with the back half of his body, the tail beats from side to side, giving him incredible power to thrust through the water. He really is beautifully *fin*ished." Mr Megamouth chuckled to himself. We all groaned.

Seymour's tail suddenly flipped from side to side and he shot to the back of the classroom.

"Why doesn't that send him all over the place?" said Laxmi.

"Ah!" said Mr Megamouth. "You mean what sailors call '*yawing*'!"

"Do I?" said Laxmi.

"Yes!" said Mr Megamouth. "He doesn't *yaw*, because he's got this!" He pointed to the big triangle-shaped fin on Seymour's back and said, "This is his dorsal fin. It's the one that sticks out of the water when he swims near the sea's surface. It keeps the front and middle of his body travelling in a straight line. It works just like the keel on a boat."

"So what are these ones for?" said Kelly, pointing to the big fins that were sticking out halfway along Seymour's body.

"Ah!" said Mr Megamouth. "They're called the pectoral fins. They're like wings. He uses them for steering, cruising and braking."

"He's got the lot, hasn't he!" said Simon. "Everything he needs to be a brilliant hunting and swimming machine."

"Exactly!" said Mr Megamouth. Then he looked at his watch and said, "Right, almost time to meet our first visitor. But before we do, I'll deflate Seymour. Just watch out for his forward thrust!" And with that he pulled the bung out of Seymour's back end. There was the most enormous thwarrrrp! noise and Seymour shot across the classroom at about a hundred miles an hour.

Goes like the wind, doesn't he!

He bounced off the stock cupboard door, and finally ended up a pathetic crumpled heap in the art corner. Two minutes later he was back in Mr Megamouth's bag of tricks!

What makes a Shark Sharky

by Laxmi Sharma and Zoe Thompson

1 Shark skeletons are made of bendy stuff called cartilage. Our noses are made of it too.

2 Shark skin is covered with little things called denticles (skin teeth). They feel rough and help protect the shark.

SHARK

scales

FISH

bony skeleton

3 Sharks don't have a fishy "swim bladder" to help them float, some sharks have to swim nearly all the time or they will sink.

4 Fish have gills so they can breathe in water. This is how they do it: the water goes in through the fishy mouth and comes out again through the gills.

WATER

There is oxygen in the water that goes into the fish's blood and the blood carries the oxygen round the fishy body.

Shark gills are different from fish. They don't have covers. They just have gill slits on the sides of their heads. They get the oxygen from the water when it flows across their gills. But the water has to be moving, so most sharks get oxygen by:

Swimming

Lying still in a current

Phew! I needed a break!

Ann Chovy and her shocking sharks

Mr Megamouth walked over to our stock cupboard and knocked twice on the door. Then this woman walked out! Or maybe I should say she swam out! She was moving her arms and legs like she was swimming breast stroke.

"Hi, kids!" she said, taking off her mask. "I'm Ann Chovy." Then, without making a sound, she opened and closed her mouth a few times, just like fish do. "I'm an ichthyologist," she continued. "That means I study fish. The ones I'm really nuts about are sharks. I'd really like to tell you about every type of shark but there isn't time so I'll just tell you about three of my favourites. We'll start with this chap!"

She turned to our big fish tank and clapped her hands. Vic and Bob, our class goldfish, disappeared and this little creature appeared . . .

"Oooer!" said Kelly. "It's glowing bright green! Is it poorly?"

"No!" said Ann. "That's the way it attracts its prey. When big sea creatures like seals, whales and dolphins see that spooky glow in the murky ocean depths they get curious and swim up to take a closer look. That's when this miniature monster strikes. Watch!"

Ann reached into her wet suit and took out a big wind-up rubber fish. She turned its key a few times, then plopped it into the tank. The moment it landed in the water the cookie-cutter dashed at it and clamped itself to its side like this:

It made a sort of suction cup with its lips then took a bite and swivelled around.

"Wow!" said Zoe. "That's just like how you cut biccy shapes out of dough."

"Which is why it's called a cookie-cutter!" said Ann, as she rescued her clockwork fish from the tank. "After the cookie-cutter has had its bite to eat the poor old victim swims off with a horrible hole in it. Sometimes the victims survive but other times the smell of blood attracts other sharks which finish them off!"

"Wow!" said Brian. "Cookie-cutters are fierce, aren't they?"

"Not half!" said Ann. "They're only 40 centimetres long but they've even attacked submarines and bitten chunks out of their rubber sound-detecting domes. Sometimes a cookie-cutter bites so hard that its teeth come out and then it swallows them with the flesh it's bitten off!"

"My gran did that," said Kelly Niblett.

"What!" said Ann. "Bit a submarine?"

"No, swallowed her false teeth!" said Kelly.

"Oh," said Ann, clapping her hands again. The cookie-cutter disappeared and Vic and Bob were suddenly back in their tank.

"OK, now for our next guest!" said Ann. "It's waiting for you over there."

She nodded towards the big sink in our art corner and we all dashed over to see what was in it. I was the first to get there.

That's not a shark! It's a dirty great rock all covered in seaweed!

"No, it's not," said Ann. "It's a wobbegong! That's the name the Australian Aborigines gave it. This one's quite young but they can grow to more than three metres long. Wobbegongs live around the coral reefs of New Guinea and Northern Australia."

"Is it dangerous?" said Laxmi.

"It is if you're a crab, fish or octopus," said Ann. "It waits half buried on the ocean floor then as they swim by it sucks them in and traps them with those needle-like teeth. But, because wobbegongs are so well camouflaged people sometimes step on them and get bitten. So let's make it vanish before your caretaker accidentally tries to bin it!"

She pulled out the sink plug and the water and the wobbegong disappeared!

"OK, now for shark number three!" said Ann. She bent over, grabbed the brass ring in the centre of a trapdoor in our classroom floor (which none of us had even noticed before!) and pulled it. Where the floor had been just a micro-second earlier there was now a huge hole full of greenish blue water. We all gasped. Then we screamed. Because *this* suddenly shot out of the hole and lay flapping around on the classroom floor!

"Quite a monster, isn't it?" said Ann "This is a Greenland shark. They live in the Arctic regions and can grow up to seven metres long. People who live in Greenland make holes in the ice, then dangle a bit of wood in the water. When the shark follows it to the surface they harpoon it. They use its skin for footwear, the oil for things like lamps and cooking, the teeth for making cutting tools and the meat for eating. The meat is poisonous. To get rid of the poison it has to be boiled lots of times and then you can eat it."

"So they *kill* them?" said Brian, looking a bit shocked.

"They do when they can," said Ann. "They have to. They depend on them for the things that help them survive. It's a bit like us turning cows into beefburgers and leather goods."

"But aren't the sharks protected?" said Laxmi.

"These aren't," said Ann. "But quite a few species are. Especially in places where they're killed in huge numbers."

"And we'll be finding out more about that later on," said Mr Megamouth.

At that moment the shark dived back under the water so Ann quickly popped the trapdoor back in place and said, "OK! That's *my* three sharks! Now it's your turn! Perhaps one of you has got a particular shark you'd like to ask me about?"

"Yes, please!" said Zoe. Then she looked at Mr Megamouth, grinned and said, "I've heard there's a shark called a megamouth! I'd like to know about that one."

"No problem!" said Ann and waved at the little stuffed fish in the glass case above our classroom door. As she did, the case began to expand and the stuffed fish started to change shape. When the fish was almost half the width of our classroom, this is what it looked like!

"That's a megamouth!" said Ann.

"Long, aren't they!" said Simon.

"Yes," said Ann. "About five and half metres. Too big to miss, you'd think. However, no one even knew they existed before 1976 when one was discovered near Hawaii, tangled up with the anchor of an American warship. When people saw its enormous mouth and its fat blubbery lips they immediately called it the megamouth!"

Mr Megamouth grinned and blushed then said, "Are we . . . sorry . . . are *they* dangerous?"

"Not to humans," said Ann. "But they are to the plankton, shrimp and jellyfish they eat.

The inside of the upper jaw of a megamouth is luminous and glows in the dark, like the cookie-cutter. Some people think this attracts their prey. Only 14 megamouths have ever been seen, but discovering them got us marine biologists really excited because it means there might well be tons more amazing unknown sharks and weird creatures at the bottom of the ocean. Which is why I'm going back down there right now!"

And with that Ann opened the trapdoor in our classroom floor again, put her face mask on, then dived into the hole and disappeared!

"Wow!" we all said.

"That was exciting, wasn't it?" said Mr Megamouth, replacing the trapdoor.

"Ace!" I said. "But what about the megamouth, Mr Megamouth?"

"No problem!" said Mr Megamouth. Then he winked at the megamouth. The megamouth winked back and a moment later it was just a stuffed freshwater fish again. "That's our trout ... without a doubt!" laughed Mr Megamouth.

I'm telling you, just about anything can happen at Pickle Hill Primary!

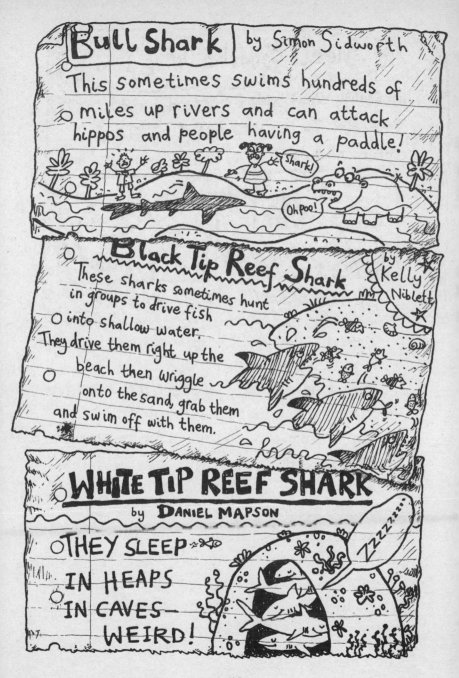

Bull Shark | by Simon Sidworth

This sometimes swims hundreds of miles up rivers and can attack hippos and people having a paddle!

Shark!

Oh poo!

Black Tip Reef Shark
by Kelly Niblett

These sharks sometimes hunt in groups to drive fish into shallow water. They drive them right up the beach then wriggle onto the sand, grab them and swim off with them.

WHITE TIP REEF SHARK
by DANIEL MAPSON

THEY SLEEP
IN HEAPS
IN CAVES—
WEIRD!

ZZZZZZZ

Swell Sharks by Charlotte Edwards

This spotty shark hides in cracks and holes in rocks. If it's attacked it swallows water and swells up so it can't be pulled out.

Great stuff! — Mr Megamouth

Dive!

"OK everyone!" said Mr Megamouth. "It's time we all took the . . . er . . . plunge too! I want you to hold your noses then pull imaginary chains like you're flushing old-fashioned loos."

We did as we were told and something amazing happened. Our whole classroom began to rock gently and two seconds later there was water lapping at the window-ledges outside. Ten seconds later the water had completely covered the big window facing the playground and the birds and bushes and buildings were going all swirly and blurry.

Twenty seconds later the birds had turned into fish, the bushes had turned into seaweed and the buildings had turned into rocks.

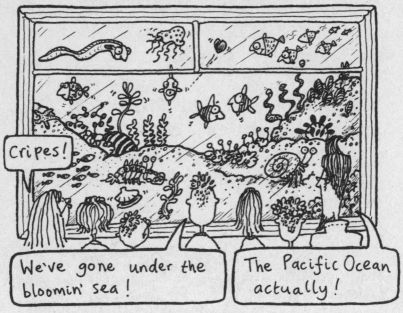

"Some of you might find this a bit scary at first. But just stay calm and whatever you do . . . DON'T open the door!" said Mr Megamouth.

"But what if we want to visit the *real* loo?" said Brian Butler.

"You'll just have to wait!" said Mr Megamouth. At that moment a huge turtle swam past the window closely followed by something large and grey with a big blunt head.

"What was *that*?" said Brian.

"A tiger shark chasing its lunch," said Mr Megamouth. "Look . . . it's back!"

It was! A ginormous shark swam up and down looking in at us. I think it must have been nearly half as long as our classroom! All of a sudden it noticed Simon Sidworth and came up to the window next to where he was sitting, then glared in at him. Simon froze. "I wanna go 'ome!" he said. "I want me mum!"

"And that tiger shark wants his dinner!" said Mr Megamouth. "But don't worry, Simon. The window has toughened safety glass to keep out thieves and vandals."

"Yeah, so stop blubberin', Simon!" said Kelly. "Here, Mr Megamouth, if that's a tiger shark, where's its stripes then?"

"They only have them when they're young," said Mr Megamouth. "This is a full-grown male and he's vicious and powerful. Along with the great white and the bull shark, divers fear them most of all. Their teeth are like tin-openers. They can bite through the shell of a sea turtle like it was a poppadom!"

Right on cue the tiger shark opened its mouth so that its horrible hooked teeth were just ten

 centimetres from Simon's nose. Simon made a little whimpering sound, and then slumped back in his chair.

"I think Simon's fainted!" said Kelly. "It's a pity I can't wack its snout with my ruler."

"It wouldn't notice," said Mr Megamouth. "Its skin is supposed to be ten times tougher than a buffalo's! But one thing you can do to them is push down on their back or their dorsal fin. It makes them stop swimming and sink to the bottom."

At that moment a diver swam into view and began rubbing on the tiger's dorsal fin.

"Bet they don't eat cat food though!" said Brian.

"I wouldn't be so sure!" said Mr Megamouth. "Despite the fact that their favourite things to eat are large fish, turtles, porpoises and seals, you'd be amazed at the other stuff that tiger sharks put away. He waved his hand and the tiger shark swam off. A moment later a lady diver appeared at the window and held up a sign that said:

The diver seemed familiar. She was! It was Mrs Platt . . . our school cook! Mrs Platt held up another sign:

These are some of the things that have been found in tiger sharks' stomachs:

And the next moment a troop of dinner ladies swam by . . . carrying this lot!:

Sack of spuds
pair of trousers
an artillery shell
a tom-tom drum

tyres
a cigar
oil drum
dynamite
an anchor

other sharks
roll of chicken wire
sea snakes
deer horns
bits of horses

"Do they ever eat people?" said Simon, who'd recovered a bit.

"Yup!" said Mr Megamouth. "And *parts* of people. A tiger shark was once caught in a fishing net and taken to an aquarium in Australia. The first thing it did was bring up its breakfast. Out came a dead rat, a bird . . . and a human arm with a rope around its wrist! The arm had a tattoo on it that the police identified as belonging to a gangster. His enemies had killed him then cut him up and put him in a box, all apart from his arm which wouldn't go in. So they tied that to a weight and threw it in the sea. If the tiger hadn't swallowed it no one would have been any the wiser!"

"Wow again!" we all said.

"People call tiger sharks the swimming dustbins of the oceans," said Mr Megamouth. "I suppose you can see why now! They really are into *junk* food aren't they!?" he snorted.

"Definitely!" I said. "But it must be terrible to have all that rubbish in your stomach. Doesn't it ever give them belly ache?"

"Well," said Mr Megamouth. "If things get *too* uncomfortable the tiger shark has a rather . . . er . . . *unusual* way of dealing with it. But I'm sure you don't want to hear about it."

"We do! We do!" said everyone. "Tell us Mr Megamouth!"

"Oh all right," said Mr Megamouth, doing a quick spin. "It turns its stomach inside out, and pushes it through its mouth. The contents spill out into the sea."

Uvvrgh, you're kidding!

"No. They really do!" said Mr Megamouth. "If they've got something like a big chunk of turtle shell inside them, it's the only way they can get rid of it. I suppose it's just like us taking the plastic bin liner out of a bin then emptying it."

"Yuk!" I said. "Sharks are weird aren't they!"

"They certainly are!" said Mr Megamouth, then he looked towards the window and said, "Uh oh! Now . . . what *have* we got here?!"

I looked where Mr Megamouth was looking . . . then gasped. Three of the *weirdest*-looking fish I'd *ever* seen were swimming towards our classroom. Mr Megamouth said they were 3.5 metres long and each one of them looked like someone had shoved a skateboard through its head sideways then stuck its eyes on either end of it! They were all swinging their huge horrible heads from side to side.

"They're members of a whole family of 'big-headed' sharks which includes bonnet sharks and wingheads," said Mr Megamouth. "These underwater nightmares you're looking at now are known as *great* hammerheads.

They're the biggest of all the hammerheads but, relatively speaking, they don't have the biggest heads. There's another hammerhead that's 1.8 metres long with a head that's nearly a metre wide!"

"Fancy having your eyes *that* far apart!" I said. I'd never seen *anything* quite like a hammerhead. "They must be looking in two directions at once!"

"They are!" said Mr Megamouth. "Their eyes are set so far apart that their brains get two completely different pictures. They have to do some pretty nifty thinking to join up the two pictures so they make sense!"

"They're so *ugly*!" said Zoe.

"Grotesque!" said Mr Megamouth.

"And why are they swinging their heads from side to side like that?" I asked.

"To see where they're going," said Mr Megamouth. "They're also looking for the catfish and stingrays they like to eat. In fact, I think that one closest to us may have just found what it's after!"

The hammerheads were all really near the ocean bed now and were swimming up and down really quickly and swinging their heads from side to side even faster.

Look at that! A huge chunk of the sea bed has just floated away!

"That isn't a chunk of sea bed," said Mr Megamouth. "It's a whopping great stingray. Or dinner, as that hammerhead probably prefers to think of it. It must have been hiding down there in the sand, hoping to avoid being seen. Ah well, too late now. Look the hammerhead's nobbled it!"

"Shouldn't that be *nailed* it?" snorted Daniel.

A hammerhead had caught the stingray and was pinning it to the sea-bed with its giant head. The stingray was twisting and turning wildly but it was well and truly trapped. Suddenly it lashed its tail and a big sort of dart thing stuck in the shark's head.

"What was *that*?" said Liam.

"The ray's using its poisonous spines to defend itself," said Mr Hammerhead, er, I mean Mr Megamouth. "But it's wasting its time. The stings are painful to humans and other creatures but they don't bother hammerheads. One was found with *96* spines in its head!"

It looked like Mr Megamouth was right. A moment after the dart entered its flesh the hammerhead quickly turned its head and took a bite out of the stingray's "wing". Ugh! I had to look away, it was eating the stingray alive!

"Aaah! Poor thing!" cried Zoe. "That's awful. It must be in *agony*!"

"But it's nature too!" said Mr Megamouth. "That stingray's done similar things to *its* victims!" He looked at his watch then said, "Anyway, seeing all this eating is making me peckish. Break's in ten minutes and today I'd like you all to stick around! Let's go!"

"Oh no!" we all said. "Do we *have* to?"

"Yes!" said Mr Megamouth. Then he grinned and said, "OK then before we do, let's see a bit more tiger action."

Our classroom began rocking gently from

side to side, then our stomachs went all queasy like when you go up fast in a lift.

"We're going up!" said Simon. "I think I'm going to puke!"

"Well," laughed Mr Megamouth. "Don't turn your stomach inside out if you do!"

Suddenly, all sorts of sea creatures went rushing past the windows, including squid, brightly coloured butterfly fish, tiger sharks, and what looked like three or four really tiny hammerheads.

Aaah! Baby hammerheads! But why aren't they with the big ones?

"They've got more sense!" said Mr Megamouth. "Lots of adult sharks eat baby sharks. That's why shark mums go somewhere quiet to give birth. Sometimes the mums even eat their own babies by mistake."

"How many sharklets do they have?" I asked.

"Actually, they're called pups," said Mr Megamouth. "And different sharks have different numbers of young. Hammerheads give birth to up to 40 pups at one time and tiger sharks can have between 10 and 80 pups."

"That's loads!" said Zoe. "How do they manage to take care of so many?"

"They don't!" said Mr Megamouth. "They leave them to fend for themselves."

"Ahh!" said Kelly. "Poor things!"

"It's not that bad," said Mr Megamouth. "As soon as they're born the pups can swim and hunt and generally look after themselves."

"That's like children going straight from the maternity hospital to their first job, then getting some shopping on the way home and cooking their own tea!" said Zoe.

"If only!" Mr Megamouth laughed.

Mr Megamouth tapped the classroom window a couple of times and as he did so the bluey green sea water outside stopped splashing and foaming and became the boring grey tarmac of our school playground. And the gorgeous sea creatures suddenly turned into screaming children.

"Looks like they started lunch break without us!" said Mr Megamouth.

SHARK BABIES

by Kelly Niblett and Simon Sidworth.

Most sharks give birth to live babies but some lay eggs.

"Mermaid's Purse"

embryo

yolk sac

dogfish shark egg

Empty sharks' eggs get washed up on beaches after storms. Sharks don't sit on their eggs like a bird does. They swim off and leave them.

Mum! Come back!

Spiral egg

Port Jackson sharks lay these. They jam them into crevices and rocks.

Most baby sand tiger sharks don't even manage to get born. While they are still in the mum, the strongest ones eat all the others until there are only two left.

mum →

Oi! You lot in there. Stop squabbling!

If they get to full size most of the sharks live to about **25** years but some live for **70** or even **100** years.

Excellent! Apparently, scientists work out how old a shark is by counting the rings on its back bones. A bit like counting the rings on a tree trunk

Mr Lee's Ocean Paradise

"Anyone going home for dinner today?" asked Mr Megamouth. When we all shook our heads he said, "Ah, that's handy!" Then, with a playful twinkle in his eye, he said, "Well, if you'll just line up I'll, er, take you down to the, er, *dining room*."

All that shark-spotting made me seriously hungry. We all lined up and I shot to the front of the queue and opened the classroom door. A couple of sailors were walking down our school corridor. Or at least we *thought* it was the corridor. Because the moment Mr

62

Megamouth led us out of the room we could see that it wasn't! We were actually on a sunny quayside full of dead smart people who all looked liked millionaires. And where our school courtyard normally is, there was this marina full of enormous motor yachts.

"Triple wow!" we all gasped as our mouths dropped open and our eyes stood out on stalks.

"Mr Megamouth!" said Kelly. "This isn't Pickle Hill. It's far too posh!"

"Well spotted, Kelly!" said Mr Megamouth, and he did a swift twizzle. "You're right, of course. We're actually in a rather smart seaside town on the west coast of America. You may be interested to know that it isn't that far from Hollywood. I thought you might like to give school dinners a miss today and have a bite by the sea instead." Then he paused, looked a bit mischievous and added, "Then again . . . maybe you won't? Just follow me!"

We did as we were told and after a few minutes' walk we came to a very smart blue building decorated with painted fish. The building's front door was behind a pair of very beautiful Chinese-style gates with leaping sharks painted on them and a sign above saying:

This looks rather nice. Let's go in!

We followed Mr Megamouth into the Ocean Paradise. It was the poshest-looking restaurant any of us had ever been in! All around the sides of the massive room people who looked like film stars were sitting at candlelit tables while in the middle there was an enormous aquarium full of all sorts of exotic fish. As we walked in a very smart waitress (who looked a bit like Mrs Platt, our school dinner lady) came up to Mr Megamouth and said, "Good afternoon, sir. How can I help you?"

"I'd like a table for 27, please," said Mr Megamouth.

The waitress sat us at a huge table and we began flipping through the menus.

In the end *everyone* decided that they'd have the shark's fin soup. That is everyone except Mr Megamouth who said he'd just have a bowl of egg fried rice.

Five minutes later the waitress brought 26 bowls of shark's fin soup and put them on the table. We were just about to tuck in when

Mr Megamouth said, "Before you start your soup, would you like to know how it came to be in front of you?"

"Er, yes, Mr Megamouth, I suppose so," said Daniel, and the rest of us all nodded.

"OK then!" said Mr Megamouth and he nodded towards the restaurant kitchen.

A second later a huge Chinese man came out carrying a massive meat cleaver.

"This is Mr Lee," said Mr Megamouth. "He's the restaurant owner and the chef. You'll tell us, won't you Mr Lee?"

"Sure fing!" said Mr Lee. Then he paused and said, "Well, in order to prepare the fins for the soup they're hung up to dry in the sun, then they're soaked and simmered to release the sharks' fin 'fibres'. These are jellyish strands which are a bit like noodles. They don't taste of much, so other things like ginger and soy sauce and dried oysters are added to them to . . . *soup* them up a bit, ha ha ha! But of course, I'm forgetting, you'll be wanting to know how they get the fins in the first place, won't you?"

Daniel looked at Mr Lee a bit suspiciously then said, "Er . . . yes?" and the rest of us all nodded again.

"Well," said Mr Lee. "To get the fins the sharks are caught in nets then hauled aboard fishing boats. Then, as the sharks flap about on the deck of the boat, the fishermen take out their big sharp knives, grab hold of them . . . and begin hacking off their fins!"

He swished his meat cleaver this way and that, to give us the general idea.

"What!" said Zoe with a look of absolute horror on her face. "While they're still *alive*!"

"Oh yes!" said Mr Lee. "It's a bit . . . er . . . *messy*! And once they're 'finned', as it's called, the sharks are thrown back into the sea. They're still alive, but of course without fins they can't swim properly. So they can't get enough oxygen and eventually drown. That's if they don't bleed to death or get ripped to pieces by other sharks."

We all looked at our bowls as if they were filled with fresh cat wee.

"Pretty terrible, isn't it?" said Mr Megamouth. "In the last ten years or so shark's fin soup has become so popular that in some places the seabed is littered with the bodies of sharks which have been 'finned'. As a way of excusing this terrible cruelty some people have even spread it about that the fins grow back again. Which is complete tosh! OK everyone, that's that then! You can tuck in now!"

For some reason I'd gone right off the idea of shark's fin soup, and I wasn't the only one!

One by one, everyone put down their spoons and pushed away their bowls.

"Well, I'm glad you all did that!" said Mr Megamouth. "One . . . because I personally think 'finning' is disgraceful. And two . . . because in this particular restaurant, shark's fin soup costs a *hundred dollars* a bowl! So you've just saved me around a couple of thousand pounds!" Then he looked at Mr Lee and said, "Could we have another 26 bowls of fried rice, please?"

"Sure fing!" said Mr Lee. He didn't seem to mind at all. Then he grinned and winked at Mr Megamouth.

Two minutes later, as we were all tucking into our fried rice, Mr Megamouth said: "Who can tell me how many people are killed by sharks each year?"

"I reckon it must be *hundreds*!" said Daniel.

"Wrong!" said Mr Megamouth. "Actually, around the whole world, no more than about 12 people are killed annually."

"Only *12* a year!" said Zoe "Is that all?"

"Yes!" said Mr Megamouth. "But do any of you know how many sharks are killed by *humans* each year?"

"Er, a *thousand*?" said Laxmi.

"No, a few more than that," said Mr Megamouth.

"Ten thousand?" said Liam.

"Well, Liam," said Mr Megamouth, "if I'd asked you how many are killed in just *one hour* . . . you'd be right. But as far as a whole year's concerned the answer is actually *one hundred million*! Or, to put it another way, more than a *quarter of a million* a day!"

"As many as that!" we all gasped. "That's *terrible*!"

"Yes it is, isn't it?" said Mr Megamouth. "Lots of them are killed because they get accidentally entangled in the nets of boats that are fishing for other sorts of fish. But others are destroyed to supply all the different things human beings want from them. And others are killed just for fun."

"How do you mean?" said Daniel.

"People catch them in big shark-fishing contests," said Mr Megamouth. "They call it sport! Afterwards, they cut off the heads for trophies and dump the bodies at the local tip. All just to prove what tough guys they are!"

"Ahh . . . that's disgusting!" gasped Simon.

"Ready for your main course, my dearies?" said a familiar voice.

We all whirled around expecting to see the Chinese waitress. But it was Mrs Platt!

"Mrs Platt!" said Daniel. "What are *you* doing in America?"

"I'm *not* in America," said our school cook. "I'm in England. At Pickle Hill Primary. And so are you!"

She was right. Somehow, while we'd all been listening to Mr Megamouth, the swanky restaurant had turned into our school dining hall and the glamorous film star look-alikes had turned into a load of chattering school kids!

Now, how about some nice fish and chips?

THE SHARK

Just to give everyone an idea of all the stuff that sharks are turned into we've drawn this ginormous shark.

SHARK MEAT: Food - cat food - farm animal food - fertilisers.

SHARK CARTILAGE: Artificial skin (for people who've been burned) - health pills - supposed to cure illnesses.

SHARK SKIN: Fashion shoes - wallets - purses - belts - jackets. In the old days it was called shagreen and the rough skin was used to smooth wood. Also to scrub ships' decks. Japanese warriors had their sword handles covered in it, to help them keep grip when they get bloody.

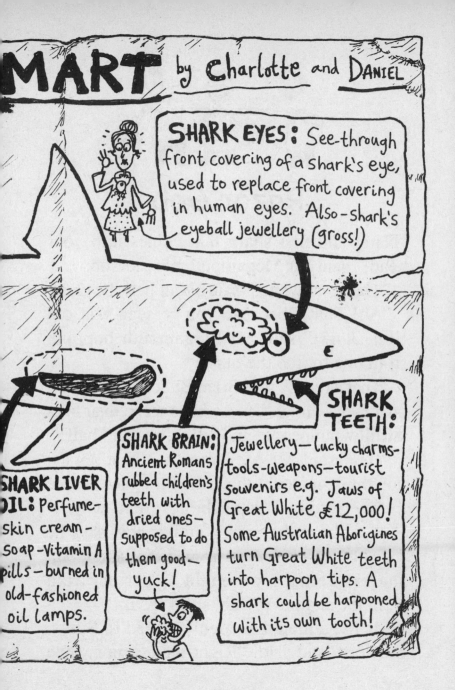

Razor Gob

"Name the first shark that comes into your head!" said Mr Megamouth next lesson.

"The great white!" said about half the class.

"Ah! That's because you've seen that old film, *Jaws*!" said Mr Megamouth hopping from one foot to the other.

"That's right!" said Brian Butler. "*I've* seen it on telly *five* times. Great whites spend their lives swallowing people and biting boats in half!"

"Ha!" said Mr Megamouth. "That's what you think, matey! I think the film gave people a few wrong ideas about great whites. Especially as the book's author now says he may have got his ideas from stories about *bull* sharks! Perhaps we ought to get the truth from the shark's mouth, so to speak!"

Mr Megamouth suddenly turned to Simon Sidworth and said, "Right then Simon, time for a change!" Then he clapped his hands.

A micro-moment later the shape of Simon's head began to alter and we all gasped. Then his arms started to shrink and he seemed to grow taller and smoother. Next, with a horrible ripping noise, an enormous shark's fin *exploded* out of the back of his shirt!

And just two seconds later Simon Sidworth was completely shark-shaped!

"Oooer, SIMON!" said Kelly, as his clothes suddenly fell off.

"Cripes!" said the rest of us.

Standing (or rather *lolling*) against Mr Megamouth's desk, where Simon had been moments earlier, was a great white shark – but with Simon's specs still perched on the end of its snout!

"Er . . . hi, Razor Gob!" said Brian. "So . . . what's it like being a great white?"

"Cool!" said Razor Gob.

"You're not as big as I thought you'd be," said Kelly. "How big *can* you grow?"

"Over six metres long!" said Razor Gob. "I'm just a young great white. My Uncle Terence was a whopping seven metres! And he weighed 1,800 kilogrammes."

"Shucks!" said Brian. "That's as heavy as a full-grown rhinoceros!"

"What's a rhinoceros?" said Razor Gob. Then he looked sad and said, "Poor old Uncle Terence got caught off the coast of California and put in the Marine Land Aquarium. He died a few days later. We hardly *ever* survive in captivity!" A little tear trickled down his cheek.

"Aaah!" said the whole class.

"Why *can't* you survive if you're captured?" said Brian.

"I'm not entirely sure," said Razor Gob. "It's probably because we can't stand being cooped up. We don't seem to know what's going on any more and we lose the will to live. I mean, if you were locked in a prison cell for the rest of your life you wouldn't like it, would you?"

"No way!" said Brian.

"What do you like best about being a great white?" I asked.

"Hunting!" said Razor Gob. "The chase is *dead* exciting! My victims hardly ever get away. See those tiny holes around my head? They're full of special jelly stuff and can detect the tiniest electrical signal. If a fish tries to hide, my detectors pick up the impulse given off by its heart beat or gill movements. So it's no use it crouching behind a big rock, 'cos I just zoom in and bite it really hard! That really stops my victim in its tracks. After that I might gobble it up or attack it again. I've got a brilliant sense of smell too! I can pick out the scent of one single drop of blood mixed up in with a thousand gallons of sea water!"

"So what do you great whites eat then, Simon . . . er I mean, Razor Gob!?" asked Zoe.

"Seals, squid, big bony fish, sea lions, dolphins, porpoises and other sharks such as makos, blues and hammerheads. We also feed off the bodies of dead whales too."

"Sometimes when we go after surface animals like sea birds and seals we just ram 'em really hard and knock 'em flying, then bite 'em while they're stunned."

"But best of all is when we leap right out of the water and land on 'em jaws first! They don't know what's hit 'em!"

Razor Gob opened his jaws really wide and began flapping his fins wildly, almost as if he was about to do one of his flying tackles!

"Ahh . . . the poor *things*!" said Kelly. "Don't you ever feel sorry for them?"

"Not really," said Razor Gob, calming down slightly. "I mean . . . if I didn't eat I couldn't survive, could I? And it's not as if I've got any choice. I'm programmed to be a meat eater and that's that! Anyway, I'd look a right softy if I went around nibbling seaweed and wimpy vegetarian stuff. All the other great whites would have a right laugh!"

"What happens if another great white turns up when you've just made a kill?" said Emily. "Do you just share it?"

"Not exactly," said Razor Gob. "We both twist about this way and that and slap our tails on the surface of the water. Whoever does the best slapping wins. If it's the other shark I share my kill with them and if it's me they can just buzz off!"

Razor Gob looked thoughtful for a moment then added. "It's not always that simple though. Sometimes us sharks get a bit carried away and if there's a big mob of us around a kill the smell of all the blood drives us all nuts and we go berserk biting anything we can. Including each other! It can be a right old ding-dong!"

"Ah!" said Mr Megamouth. "That's what the ichthyologists call a 'feeding frenzy'."

"What's an itchy wajjamacallit then?" said Razor Gob.

"Someone who studies fish like Miss Chovy who came to see us earlier," said Laxmi.

"I wonder what *they* taste like?" said Razor Gob.

"What was the last thing you had to eat?" said Zoe.

"Oh, a young seal pup I caught about about a week ago," said Razor Gob.

"A week!" we all said.

"Yeah!" said Razor Gob. "Us great whites can go *ages* between meals. A big sea lion or a porpoise will keep us going a month or more!"

"Do your victims ever fight back?" said Kelly.

"I once had a scrap with a elephant seal. I think I bit off more than I could chew. Its tooth just missed my eye. It's lucky I can roll them back inside my head. Look!"

Razor Gob rolled his eyeballs up so just the whites were showing . . . like this:

"Hey!" said Razor Gob. "Tell you what else I can do! I can swim along with my head lifted right out of the water and my gob wide open so you can see all of my teeth. It looks really cool! All us great whites can do it! It frightens the life out of people. Ha!"

"Ah!" said Mr Megamouth. "That would be what the scientists call 'gaping'."

Razor Gob 3

"Do they?" said Razor Gob. "Well, I don't know about that but I did it just next to a boat full of tourists last week and they nearly shot out of their skins. Cor . . . you should have heard them all scream! That's me though . . . anything for a laugh!"

"Do great whites eat people much?" said Brian.

"Hardly ever!" said Razor Gob. "Uncle Terence once mistook a surfer for a seal and knocked him off his board. Took a snap at him but missed. Actually, Uncle Terence once tried to eat *me*!"

"Er, Razor Gob?" said Liam a little bit nervously. "Erm, have *you* . . . er ever eaten a . . . person!?"

"No, never!" Razor Gob. "But I suppose there's always a first time. Actually I'm feeling a bit peckish right now!"

As Razor Gob said this he leaned towards Liam who looked absolutely terrified. Razor Gob carried on leaning until the tip of his snout was almost touching the end of Liam's nose.

But, just when it looked like Razor Gob might actually open his huge jaws and take a bite out of Liam, he suddenly began to quiver all over. Then, a second after that, his huge and powerful body began to turn back into the weedy pathetic body of Simon Sidworth. And a moment after that . . . he *was* Simon Sidworth! Simon blinked a couple of times, then, noticing that he was wearing only his undies, he blushed a deep shade of coral pink.

"Oh, hi, Liam!" he said, peering at Liam through his steamed up specs.

"Hi, Simon," said Liam, breathing a sigh of relief. "N . . . n . . . nice to have you back!"

Razor Gob's Camouflage

by Zoe Thompson

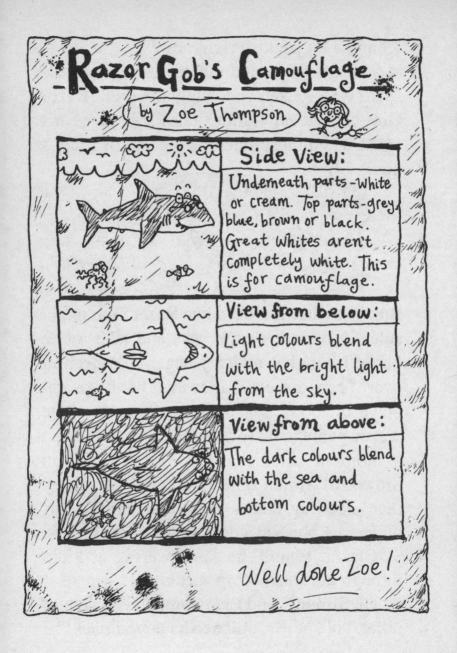

Side View:
Underneath parts - white or cream. Top parts - grey, blue, brown or black. Great Whites aren't completely white. This is for camouflage.

View from below:
Light colours blend with the bright light from the sky.

View from above:
The dark colours blend with the sea and bottom colours.

Well done Zoe!

Wish you were here

After Simon had got himself dressed, Mr Megamouth took a postcard out of his desk drawer and held it up so we could all see it. It was a photograph of a sunny beach full of happy people. At the front of the picture a really sun-tanned man was standing in the surf, grinning at the camera.

"Zoe got this postcard from her cousin in Sydney," said Mr Megamouth. "That chap at the front's an Australian lifeguard."

"S'right!" the man in the photograph said suddenly, making us all jump out of our skins. "My name's Kev. Hey, you pommy rugrats! Why don't you all come down under and take a squizz at an Ozzie beach! Just do what it says on the card!"

We all looked at the card, which said:

Greetings from BONDI BEACH Wish you were here!

"Go on then!" said Mr Megamouth. "Wish you were *there!*"

"OK!" we all yelled. "We wish we were . . . *there!*" and a second later we found ourselves on the hot golden sand, listening to the crashing surf and the happy shouts of the beach people.

"Wow!" we all gasped. "We got *here* quick!"

"Certainly beats 26 hours on a jet!" said Mr Megamouth. "I must try it more often. I wish I'd brought my cozzie!"

"Mr Megamouth tells me you wanna know all about after-darks!" said Kev.

"No!" said Simon. "Sharks actually!"

"Ha!" laughed Kev. "You little pommy fruit loop! *After-darks* is our Oz nickname for sharks. And I'm the bloke to ask about them! As well as saving drongos who get into trouble in the surf, it's my job to look out for sharks. Sometimes I walk up and down keeping me eyes skinned and sometimes I sit at the top of me observation tower. As well as me there's the pilot in that spotter plane up there."

"Soon as we spy a shark, we sound the alarm and everyone rattles their dags and gets out of the water real fast. Apart from the crazy surfies. If they've got themselves a really good wave sometimes even a shark won't make them give it up! Talk about shark biscuits! Right . . . question time! Fire away, sticky beaks!"

"Er, what's a shark biscuit?" I asked.

"It's what we call a young or inexperienced surfer," said Kev. "Because they're the one's most likely to end up as snacks for sharks!"

"Just how dangerous are sharks?" said Liam.

"Varies!" said Kev. "If you're a fish, a seabird, a seal or any other sort of marine animal you better watch out! But if you're human you aren't in nearly so much danger. Of the 400 types of shark about 30 of them are known to be dangerous to man. Your chance of being attacked by a shark is about 300 million to one. More people die in car crashes in one single month than have been killed by *all* the shark attacks in recorded history. Every year, elephants kill *ten times* more people than sharks do! And do you see people screaming with terror every time they see an elephant? No . . . they generally think they're big friendly softies, don't they?!"

"So if we wanted to go in the sea right now, would we be safe?" asked Zoe.

"Ah!" said Kev. "You probably would be here, because we've got shark nets stretched across the bay to keep sharks away from the swimming area. But you still need to be careful because you're never *entirely* safe! Around the world there are about 100 reported shark attacks on people every year and between two and 15 of them are fatal. A fair few of these attacks happen here in Oz!"

"Do you know any stories about them?" said Liam.

"I guess I do!" said Kev. "Surely you don't want to hear one!?"

"Yes, we *do*!" said everyone.

"Well, let me see now," said Kev, scratching his head. "One that comes to mind immediately is the story of a 13-year-old lad called Raymond Short."

As Kev spoke, he waggled his fingers and the scene behind him changed. It was still a beach but it was a *different* beach from the one we were sitting on and we were suddenly looking at a huge postcard-shaped cinema screen!

That's young Raymond. He was swimming when this great white with a very bad attack of the hungies grabs hold of his leg!

Raymond screams fit to bust and everyone sees he's in strife so half a dozen life-savers go belting into the surf, grab hold of him, then carry him out.

Except, as they do, they see that the shark is still hanging on to the other end of him.

It was only when they got him right out of the water and began levering its mouth open that the shark finally let go of his leg.

"Strewth!" said Kev as the scene faded. "I reckon that after-dark must have been so hungry it could have eaten a horse, then chased the jockey! Later on, when the boffins were having a squizz at its body, they saw that it was quite badly injured so they more or less worked out that it wasn't fit enough to catch its normal food. Which is probably why it attacked Raymond!"

"Cor!" said Liam. "That was an amazing story, Kev. I suppose the best way not to get attacked is never to go in the deep water! Or even in the water at all!"

"Ha! Don't be so sure, mate!" laughed Kev. "First off, more than half of shark attacks take place in less than five feet of water. And sometimes sharks come right *out* of the water to get their victims!" He waggled his fingers again and a new giant movie-postcard appeared. . .

Back in 1972 a woman was paddling on Taperoo Beach in South Oz. All of a sudden, this two-metre shark came charging at her like a rocket.

She legged it out of the sea and just kept going up the beach. And so did the shark! It was going so fast that it shot up the sand behind her.

In the end it did stop and that was when the lifeguards raced in and clobbered it with a hammer!

"Wow!" we said, as the scene faded and we all moved further away from the water.

"What's your chance of surviving a shark attack?" said Zoe as the giant postcard disappeared.

"Much, much better than it used to be!" said Kev. "In the old days you'd probably bleed to death or die of infection. But nowadays there's blokes like me and whizzo medics around to look after you and get you to the hospital in two shakes of a lamb's tail. And even if you lose a limb to a shark you can have a falsy! And how's this. There was one bloke lost his left leg to a shark . . . twice!"

"There was this diver called Henri Bource," explained Kev. "In 1964 he was attacked by a great white which bit off his left leg. He eventually recovered from his wounds and had an artificial leg fitted so he could start diving again. Some time after this *another* great white attacked him and bit off his *false* left leg!"

Kev looked up and down the beach, then said: "OK! Just a few more questions, then I'll have to rattle me dags or me mates'll think I'm chucking a berko. That's skiving to you Pommies!"

"Is it true that more men get attacked than women?" said Mr Megamouth.

"Sure is!" said Kev. "Women go in the sea just as much as men but the sharks prefer biting the fellahs! About eight times as much as the girls, I've heard! People think it's because the blokes are forever leaping around acting tough."

"If you do get attacked what should you do?" said Laxmi.

"Difficult one, that!" said Kev. "People try all sorts. Punching the shark on the nose. Gouging its eyes with their thumbs. But of course the best thing is to have a mate around to help you. Or a lifeguard like me." Then he laughed and said, "Failing that, a dolphin might come in useful!"

"A dolphin?!" said Daniel. "How do you mean?

"Well," said Kev, twitching his fingers, "there are quite a few stories about dolphins saving people from after-darks. This is my favourite one!"

Back in 1989 three young lads were surfing off the coast of New South Wales with a load of dolphins. All of a sudden the dolphins got real twitchy and began milling around just below the lads' surf boards.

A second later this three-metre great White comes zooming in and slams straight into one of the boys. It bit a great chunk out of his surfboard and a fair-sized bite out of him!

Next mo', the dolphins began splashing about and ramming into the shark. Eventually it swam off and the lads escaped.

"Wow," laughed Mr Megamouth. "That's quite a story. Thank you, Kev!"

But suddenly Kev wasn't there. Nor was the sand and the sea.

"Oh, palpitating pilchards!" said Mr Megamouth. "I was enjoying that. And I was hoping for a paddle too."

Seven Shark Safety Tips
by Liam O'Brady and Charlotte Edwards

1 Don't swim at dusk or at night. That's mainly when they hunt. They aren't called 'after-darks' just because it rhymes!

2 Don't swim on your own. Stay with a mate... or a bunch of mates.

3 Don't swim if you've got an open cut. Sharks can smell blood from over a mile away.

4 Don't wee in the sea! It attracts them.

5 If there are shoals of fish near you keep an eye on them. If you notice them getting a bit panicky or bunching up it could be because there's a shark about.

6 Don't swim with pets or other animals. They attract sharks by splashing.

7 Don't swim near anyone who is fishing or spear fishing.

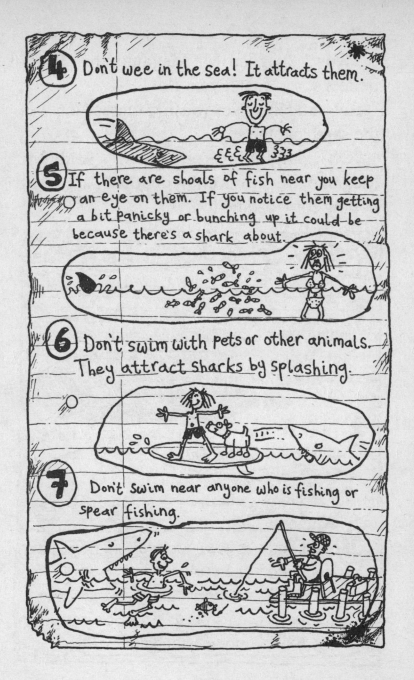

The shark fighter

When we all came in from afternoon break, Mr Megamouth was sitting in front of a huge world globe and spinning it absentmindedly.

"OK, tribe!" he said. "Gather round my gobsmacking globe! We're going to find out a bit about what people from the past thought of sharks. We'll start with the ones who picked fights with them. We know for certain it happened on islands in the Pacific Ocean. Does anyone know where that is?"

I looked at the globe, pointed to a huge blue patch and said, "Is that it?"

"Well done, Charlotte," said Mr Megamouth. "Now, what I want you to do is to put your finger on that group of islands there."

I did as I was told.

"Good!" said Mr Megamouth, then he clicked his fingers. As he did, the blue, green and brown faded from the globe and its whole surface went completely see-through!

I was closest, of course, so I could see what was happening. "Look, everyone!" I shouted. "I can see Hawaii!"

Inside the globe we could see the shoreline of the island. Joined on to it was a big pool with walls made of rocks. There was a gap in the rocks where it went into the sea. Huge crowds were gathered on the walls and some people were throwing chunks of meat and whole fish into the pool.

"Looks like some sort of arena," said Liam.

"It is!" said Mr Megamouth.

Suddenly a black fin appeared at the entrance to the arena. It circled a couple of times, then sped into the middle. As it did a really tough-looking man wearing only a loin cloth slid into the shallow water and waded towards the fin.

"What is he?" said Brian.

"A fighter!" said Mr Megamouth. "He's going to take on the shark."

"You're kidding!" said Daniel.

"No, I'm not," said Mr Megamouth. "In Spain they have toreadors who fight bulls. In ancient Rome they had people who fought all sorts of wild beasts. In ancient Hawaii they had people who did battle with sharks. It was to entertain the kings."

"What's he going to fight it with?" said Kelly.

"A single shark's tooth," said Mr Megamouth. "It's on that piece of wood which he's holding in his fist. But he can't use it straight away. The rules say he has to let the shark charge at him first. Then, at the last moment, he must dive beneath it and attempt to stab its stomach with the tooth."

"It's attacking! It's attacking!" screamed Kelly.

It was! The sinister fin was racing towards the man. The moment it reached him the water around him started bubbling. Suddenly, the shark leapt right out of the water. As it did the man went into a crouch, grasping his shark tooth in readiness to stab it. But at the last minute the shark flipped to one side, leaving the man jabbing at thin air.

"Ah!" said Mr Megamouth. "Looks like he's not going to make it!"

"How do you know?" I asked, feeling more than a little bit queasy.

"The shark's disappeared under the water. He can move really fast. . ."

As Mr Megamouth spoke, the scene began to fade from the globe and bit by bit the countries and oceans began to reappear on its surface.

"Did people really fight sharks?" I asked. I couldn't believe what I'd just seen.

"Yes they did," said Mr Megamouth. "That arena you saw there was actually found by the Americans when they were building a huge dock at Pearl Harbour in the 1900s."

"So there was cruelty to sharks even then?" asked Kelly, remembering the shark's fin soup episode.

"Yes. But some islanders worshipped sharks," said Mr Megamouth. "They made sacred caves for their shark gods to live in, and sacrificed human victims on huge altars they built in the caves."

"Oh, yuk," we all shouted.

"Life was tough for people too," said Mr Megamouth. "But they told some wonderful sharky stories!"

When they were out of sight he took a short cut to the sea.

As soon as they went into the ocean he ate them.

Munch! Munch!

Aggh! Help!

In the end a brave warrior killed Kamaikaahui and was rewarded by being allowed to marry the chief's daughter.

.THE END.

Excellent work, you two. Did you know that in Sri Lanka they used shark charmers to stop the sharks attacking people who were diving for pearls?

Captain Codpiece

Mr Megamouth glanced up at the oil painting of a gnarled old sea captain that hangs at the back of our classroom. He's steering a ship through giant waves and the picture's called "Weathering the storm". It must have been up there for yonks!

Weathering the storm

"Captain Codpiece!" said Mr Megamouth to the picture. "What can *you* tell us about sharks?" One of the old sea dog's eyebrows twitched!

Then his mouth opened, and he *spoke*! "Ahoy there, Megamouth, yer big lazy landlubber!" he growled. "Sure! I can tell yer a yarn or three about them pesky wolves of the sea!"

The next moment the Captain climbed out of the picture and walked over to Mr Megamouth's desk, leaving a trail of sea water across the classroom floor.

"Cripes!" we all gasped, as he perched himself on the edge of the desk and said, "Listen, shipmates, I've sailed seven seas and explored *oodles* of oceans! And I've seen a few sharking sights in me time and 'eard tell of a fair few more! Just you keep an eye on that picture up there and you'll see what I mean."

We looked up at the picture and, as we did, Captain Codpiece's ship sailed out of view and was replaced by a really old-fashioned sailing ship which was being driven on to rocks by huge waves.

"Now!" said the Captain. "That there's an ancient Greek sailing ship in a bit of trouble. Those poor ol' sailors you can see jumping overboard, they're gonna get grabbed by sharks."

"Uuurgh!" we all said at once.

"'Orrible, isn't it?" said Captain Codpiece. "We know about all that stuff because a Greek historian called Herodotus wrote about it back in the 5th century. But he didn't call them 'sharks'. He said them vicious fishes were sea monsters."

"In 16th-century England nobody had even heard the word shark until Captain Sir John Hawkins came back from his Caribbean battles with the Spanish and told of lots of his sailors being eaten by strange things called sharks. The experts reckon that Captain Hawkins and his men learned the word *shark* from the Mayans what lived in Central America. The Mayans called them ferocious fishes chioc or xioc, which was their word for *fury*! And that sounds just like *shark* when you say it, don't it?"

Captain Codpiece stroked his huge white beard thoughtfully for a moment, then said: "Now here's a tale for you! In the 18th century a 14-year-old cabin boy called Brook Watson had his leg bitten off by a shark. When he grew up he became Lord Mayor of London and he had his missing leg stuck on his coat of arms.

The Captain suddenly looked all serious and then said, "One of the most sharking times for sailors was World War II. For instance, when the American warship *Indianapolis* got torpedoed by a Japanese sub, 1,200 sailors jumped into the sea but only 316 of them survived!"

"Why?" said Brian.

"'Cos the sharks got the rest, o' course!" said Captain Codpiece. "The survivors said how as they could see packs on 'em circling around in the clear water 25 feet below 'em and 'ow as they'd suddenly shoot up to the surface and just grab a bloke then tear off his. . ."

"That's quite enough, thank you, Captain." said Mr Megamouth.

"Suit yerself!" said the Captain. "Right, crew! Anyone want to ask me a question?"

"Yes, please, Captain Codswallop!" said Simon Sidworth. "What's the biggest shark in the world? The great white?"

"No way!" roared Captain Codpiece. "Next to the biggest shark in the world, the great white's a tiddler. The biggest shark in the world is the whale shark. But don't go getting your bellbottoms in a twist over its name. 'Cos it definitely *ain't* no whale! It's only called that 'cos it's so flippin' big. It's a shark! An' it's massive!"

Captain Codpiece suddenly looked excited, then said, "Look! I tell you what. Let's set sail an' see if we can manage to get a gander at one!"

"But we haven't got a boat!" said Simon.

"Yes, we 'ave!" said Captain Codpiece. "Just you lot pull these desks together an' me and Megamouth'll set the ocean in motion!"

Two minutes later we'd pushed all our desks together, then piled our chairs on top of them. While we did that, Captain Codpiece and Mr Megamouth got busy getting buckets of water from the art corner sink and sloshing them around the classroom floor.

"Right! All aboard the *Dolphin*!" cried Captain Codpiece as he emptied his last bucket. We all clambered up on to our chairs and Captain Codpiece began handing out life jackets.

Come on, Megamouth! Shake a leg!

Ay, ay, Cap'n!

Mr Megamouth did one of his daft twizzles and scrambled up on to the last empty chair.

At that moment the water began to rise really quickly until it had almost covered the legs of our tables. Except our tables weren't tables any more. They'd joined together and become a large wooden ship which was now rocking wildly as the water level crept up more and more rapidly. And as the water went up . . . *we* went up. Up and up, until just when it seemed we would all be squashed between our "boat" and the ceiling, it began floating

towards the "Weathering the storm" picture.

The moment we reached the painting the classroom ceiling suddenly wasn't there any more! The walls and windows had disappeared too! We were staring across a huge ocean listening to the sea birds that swooped around us. Next we heard an engine roar into life and saw that Captain Codpiece was scanning the horizon at the front of the *Dolphin*. He turned and grinned at us.

And with that the *Dolphin* began to move forward.

Soon we were rocking and bouncing our way across the water as the huge waves slapped at our bow and great showers of salt spray splashed over us.

"Er . . . Captain Codpiece," I asked. "Where are we?"

"Somewhere in the Pacific Ocean," cried the Captain. "I think it's time to do a bit of shark-spotting! Keep your eyes peeled"

"Ay, ay, Cap'n!" we all yelled. Then we stood up, shaded our eyes with our hands and began squinting out to sea in the hope that we'd be the first to spot a shark.

They'll be dancing the hornpipe next!

After about five minutes, Daniel suddenly cried, "Look! There's a sunken ship over there! It must have capsized."

We all looked to where Daniel was pointing and saw what looked like the hull of an upturned boat, floating in the water about a hundred metres away from us. But as we stared it twitched a couple of times then began moving towards us.

"That isn't a ship!" said Mr Megamouth. "It's a whale shark."

"Oh, no!" gasped Simon. "It's humongous! Are we in danger?!"

"Don't worry, you young shrimp!" laughed Captain Codpiece. "These critters are big softies. They are huge though!"

The whale shark had now swum up close to the *Dolphin* and in the beautiful clear water we could now see its dark skin which was covered with lovely yellowish white spots and stripes.

"She's a biggy!" said Captain Codpiece. "A 50-footer, I reckon!"

"That's longer than a bus! Or six table tennis tables!" said Simon.

"Well," said Mr Megamouth. "They *are* the biggest fish in the world!"

"We'll just edge up a bit closer," said Captain Codpiece.

"Don't you think we might hurt it if we knock into it?" said Chantelle.

"No fear of that!" said Captain Codpiece. "They're tough critters. Their skin is really thick. It's got a 14-centimetre layer of gristle under it that makes it as strong as a steel-braced truck tyre. Why, back in the old days I saw fellahs try to kill 'em with guns and harpoons. But they just tightened up the muscles under their skin and the bullets and spears bounced off! Now I think back on it, it seems awful cruel, seeing as the whale shark is so docile and harmless. They're so friendly. I've even seen divers hanging on to their fins, hitching a ride. But if you touch 'em on the tail, they dive immediately!"

Just as we got within about two metres of the whale shark it opened its mouth.

"How obliging," said Mr Megamouth. "You obviously want to show us those fantastic teeth of yours."

"What teeth?" said Liam. "I can't see any."

"Look closely!" said Mr Megamouth. "You're not looking for big slashers and sawers.

"These are tiny filterers. It's got between 30,000 and 50,000 of them! They strain food from the water. Stuff like the tiny plants and animals known as plankton. And squid, anchovies and sardines."

The whale shark's mouth must have been at least a metre and half wide. As we all stared at its thousands of tiny little teeth, it dipped its head and made a scooping movement.

"Look! It's sucking in water now," said Mr Megamouth. "In the next hour it'll probably filter enough H_2O to fill a big swimming pool."

When the whale shark had finished sucking in sea water it swam right next to the *Dolphin* and began rubbing itself against the hull of the boat. As it did so, everyone leaned over the side and clicked their tongues at it as if it was a pet budgie.

"Can I pat it?" said Simon, suddenly getting all courageous.

"Course you can, young shrimp!" said Captain Codpiece. "Just make sure you. . ."

It was the big wave that caused Simon to fall into the sea. Just as he was reaching out to stroke the shark, the water hit the *Dolphin* and rocked it so violently that Simon was there one minute and gone the next. Kelly immediately put her hand up and said, "Er, 'scuse me, Mr Megamouth. Simon's in the sea with the shark."

"I can see he is," said Mr Megamouth. "It's lucky he's wearing that life jacket."

"He doesn't seem worried, does he?" said the Captain.

"No, he seems quite happy," said Mr Megamouth. "Look, he's cadging a ride now. Just let's hope it doesn't take him too far away."

The whale shark was still on the surface and after patting it a couple of times Simon had grabbed one of its fins. It didn't dash off or dive to the sea bed with him but just began swimming around and around, with the *Dolphin* in tow. After they'd done six or seven laps, Simon let go of his new friend and gave us all the thumbs-up sign. A moment later, the shark gently flicked its huge tail fin and plunged back down to the mysterious depths of the Pacific Ocean.

"Wow!" said Simon, as Captain Codpiece hauled him back on board. "That was unbelievable. I think I'll probably be a deep-sea diver when I grow up, or maybe one of those itchy-flea-ologists!"

So that was that! Simon had a ride on a whale shark, we all saw the biggest fish in the world and then, suddenly, our final adventure was over. The Pacific Ocean was now just a puddle on the classroom floor, we were sitting on chairs on tabletops, all completely high and dry (except for Simon, that is), and Captain Codpiece gave us a final wave and walked back into his picture.

"School's just finishing!" said Mr Megamouth, pointing to our classroom window. "Look, everyone's going home."

"I bet they'll be dead jealous when they find out where we've been!" said Laxmi, taking off her life jacket.

"I shouldn't worry about that," said Mr Megamouth. "Don't forget. They all have their adventures too!"

Simon was still attempting to wring out his wet shirt while the rest of us packed our bags. "I think I'll be hooked on sharks for the rest of my . . . *Oh no!*" His face suddenly went as pale as a great white's underbelly. "Jumping jellyfish!" he gasped. "There's my *mum!*"

We all followed the direction of his gaze and saw Mrs Sidworth striding across the playground.

"She's supposed to be taking me to the dentist!" said Simon. "If she sees me like this she'll go shark raving bonkers!"

But it was too late. Simon's mum was already in the doorway.

"Simon!" she barked. "Why *on earth* are you soaking wet!? And *what's* happened to your shirt. And what's *that* in your hair? It looks like . . . *seaweed!*"

Er... er, well, mum. It's a long stor...

But before he could say any more his mum had spotted Mr Megamouth and marched straight up to him.

"Mr Megamouth!" she barked. "Perhaps *you'd* like to tell me why my Simon looks like he's been dragged through an aquarium backwards?"

"Well," spluttered Mr Megamouth. "I'd really like to help you, Mrs Sidworth. But, as it happens, I'm playing in a really important water polo match in just ten minutes. And I don't want to be late for it. So I really must dash!"

And with that, he did three of his twizzles, grabbed his bag of tricks, then dashed from the room and disappeared.